The Little
VAN GOGH

Catherine de Duve

Vincent van Gogh was born on March 30, 1853, in the village of Groot Zundert in Holland. His father, Theodorus, was a Protestant minister. Vincent was the oldest of six children. He had two brothers and three sisters. He was especially close to his younger brother, Theo. At 16, Vincent left school and went to work for his uncle Cent, who was an art dealer. Vincent visited many museums and admired the works of the great masters. After seven years, he decided to move to the Borinage, a poor mining region in Belgium, to serve as a lay minister. The miners there did not have much money, and their children had to work in the fields or the mines rather than go to school. Vincent taught them stories from the Bible.

Vincent

.. AN ARTIST

When Vincent was 27, he decided to become an artist, but he didn't know if he had any talent. He began by drawing in his sketchbook and making copies of famous paintings. His first paintings were of hard-working country people - miners, peasants, *peat workers* and artisans.

Peat Worker: *someone who makes poor-quality fuel and fertilizer from peat moss.*

See how Vincent's art changed over ten years.

1880	1882	1883	1885
1886	1887	1887	1888
1889	1889	1890	1890

PEASANTS

In this small cottage, everything is dark and quiet. The oil lamp weakly lights the peasants' tired faces. To eat their meagre meal of potatoes, the family shares a single fork and eats from one big plate. What do you think they are drinking?

 Can you find 5 cups? 2 coffee pots? 2 bonnets? A clock?

This was Vincent's first major painting. He wanted to show what life was like for poor peasants. Why do you think he painted with dark earth tones?

Years later, Vincent painted peasants in the South of France. With their shoes kicked off, they nap in the shade of the haystacks after a long, hot morning's work of harvesting hay.

How are the French harvesters different from the Dutch peasants? What kinds of clothes, hats, and shoes are they wearing?

MONTMARTRE

In the spring of 1886, Vincent moved to France. For the next two years, he lived with his younger brother, Theo, in a small apartment in Montmartre, a part of Paris where many artists lived. Vincent met other artists there. Some of them were impressionists. Others painted in a style called pointillism, in which each painting is made with thousands of tiny dots of colour. At first, Vincent found these new styles of art to be odd-looking, with strange colours. But soon, he wanted to flood his own paintings with light and bright colours too. He even made some paintings with tiny dots and others in the style of the impressionists.

View from Theo's Apartment in Paris, 1887

Today Montmartre is a busy part of Paris, but in Van Gogh's time it was almost in the country. Vincent loved to paint the gardens, windmills, and Parisians out for a Sunday stroll. One windmill was so small, people called it "the pepper mill." Children loved Montmartre's littlest windmill!

Which of these paintings is in the pointillist style (with tiny dots) and which is in the impressionist style?

SELF-PORTRAITS

Vincent liked to visit the Louvre Museum in Paris. He particularly admired the portraits by Rembrandt, a famous Dutch painter. He wanted to make portraits too. Unfortunately, Vincent didn't have enough money to pay a model to pose for him.

Vincent had an idea. "I'll look in the mirror and paint what I see. That won't cost me anything!" In the next five years, he painted at least 37 self-portraits.

Vincent's self-portraits are often from the chest up. Why do you think that is?

Draw your own self-portrait with Vincent's famous straw hat.

Van Gogh

Vincent may have visited the Louvre for inspiration, but it was in an art supply shop in Paris that he discovered Japanese art. He particularly admired the prints of Hiroshige, a Japanese artist. They were unlike anything he had ever seen. Vincent loved the Japanese depictions of mountains, trees, flowers, and ladies in traditional kimonos. Like many young artists of the time, Vincent was entranced by the style of Japanese art, with its strong lines and pure colours.

Kimo

Like Van Gogh, create your own drawing based on Hiroshige's print.

Hiroshige

Pere Tanguy had an art supply shop in Montmartre. He helped young artists by accepting their paintings as payment for art supplies. Vincent painted Tanguy sitting in a room covered with Japanese prints.

Can you find 3 women in kimonos? Flowers? A green hillside?

WHAT COLOURS?

To show people that he was a serious artist, Vincent sometimes painted himself in front of an easel, holding a palette and brushes. In each self-portrait he painted, he wanted to capture his character and his emotions with each brushstroke. He looked in the mirror and asked himself, "Which colours and patterns will express who I am and how I feel?"

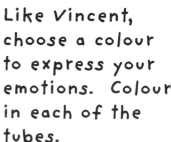

Like Vincent, choose a colour to express your emotions. Colour in each of the tubes.

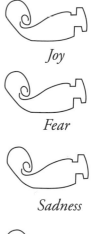

Joy

Fear

Sadness

Friendship

Before paint tubes became available in 1863, artists had to mix their own paints. They bought coloured powders and mixed them with oil. When paint tubes were invented, it became easier for artists to go on outdoor painting trips.

Every detail shows Vincent's unique style. Notice the many different brushstrokes that he used. Can you find his painting materials in his self-portrait?

Jacket

Canvas back

Palette

Paint brushes

Oil paints

Jars of paint thinner and paint drying solution

SPRING

When Theo and his wife had a baby, Vincent gave them this painting.

In early 1888, Vincent left Paris for the South of France. He wanted to find a tranquil place in the country to paint. As he travelled south, the countryside was covered with snow, but spring was coming. When the trees began to bloom he painted this picture. The flowering trees reminded him of the Japanese art he loved so much. Vincent settled in the town of Arles. He took a room in a hotel near the train station. His brother Theo sent him art supplies and some money to live on.

Vincent sent Theo his paintings to sell, but sadly, Theo was unable to sell a single one. That spring, Vincent made 14 paintings of blooming fruit trees. He worked with great passion and eagerness and would sometimes paint several works of art in a single day. In two years, Vincent completed over two hundred paintings!

Peach tree in bloom.

Colour the tree branch and its flowers.

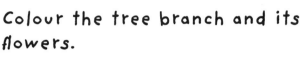

In Arles, Vincent rented a yellow house. He had long dreamt of forming a community of artists who would live and paint together. He hoped they would inspire one another and invent a new style of art. He invited his artist friends to join him in the South of France, but only one came: Paul Gauguin. Vincent was excited that Gauguin was coming to live with him. "How wonderful it will be to paint together and share our ideas," Vincent thought.

Vincent's yellow house on the corner had green shutters and a green door. Yellow was his favourite colour. For him, it represented sunshine, joy and friendship. Here he painted the street and sidewalk yellow, too. People stroll by his house as others sit in a nearby sidewalk café. A train passes in the distance. Can you see its white steam?

Find these details in the painting. How many shades of yellow do you see?

Inside the yellow house, there were four rooms. Downstairs there was a kitchen and a studio for painting. Upstairs there were two bedrooms. Vincent wanted his bedroom to be the perfect place to relax, read, and write. He found simple furniture for the room and hung his paintings on the walls.

In France in the 1800s, many homes did not have indoor bathrooms. People kept a pitcher of water and a washbasin in their bedrooms to wash themselves. What else do you see on Vincent's wash table? Can you find his straw hat and blue jacket hanging on hooks near the bed? Where do you suppose the two doors lead?

How many differences can you find between the two paintings of Van Gogh's Bedroom?

NIGHT COLOURS

Van Gogh painted a night scene filled with light. Stars shine in the sky and gas lanterns light the café terrace and the street in front of it. A waiter serves customers as couples walk along the cobblestone street. The whole block is filled with different colours. In the distance, a horse-drawn carriage comes our way - can you hear the horse's hooves on the cobblestones?

Vincent loved to paint at night. It is said that he sometimes put candles on his hat and easel to see what he was painting.

"It often seems to me that the night is even more richly coloured than the day."

Meanwhile, in the café at the railroad station, people huddle over their drinks. A billiard table sits in the middle of the room, but no one is playing. Harsh lights glare down on the melancholy scene. When Vincent painted The Night Café, he felt lonely. He used contrasting reds and greens, and strong yellows, to create the unsettling scene. How do the colours and lighting, the empty chairs and messy tables make you feel?

Which of the two cafés would you like to visit?

All his life, Vincent was poor, but he had friends who believed in his art. His brother Theo was his best friend. An art dealer in Paris, Theo supported and encouraged Vincent, and tried to sell his paintings. Vincent's friends often served as his models. He painted writers, artists, poets, peasants, soldiers, housewives, and others. One of these women ran the café at the railroad station. The other was the postman's wife.

What do you think it would have been like to sit for a portrait for Van Gogh?

In Arles, Vincent made friends with the Roulin family. This is Joseph Roulin, who worked as a postman. He is wearing his uniform. His wife is the lady in green. Vincent liked to paint portraits of Roulin. He once said that the postman reminded him of the great Greek philosopher, Socrates. Roulin was a very interesting man. Does Vincent show that in his portrait?

A philosopher is a wise man who thinks deeply about life, nature, and man's place in the universe.

FISHING BOATS

One day, Vincent walked alone for hours until he reached the sea. There he came upon four small sailboats on the shore. They reminded him of the fishing boats of his childhood in Holland. Suddenly he was homesick for his friends and family. He sketched the boats, naming one Amitie, meaning friendship. Vincent wrote, "These boats have such beautiful colours, they remind me of flowers."

Vincent sketched the boats and later painted two versions, one
with oil paint and one in watercolour.

Colour the picture with your favourite art technique:

ink

oil paint

watercolour

FLOWERS

Sunflowers were Vincent's favourite flower. Big and yellow, they reminded him of the sun and cheered him when he felt sad and lonely. When Vincent painted sunflower pictures, he worked fast, using thick, rapid brushstrokes going in all different directions. He painted lots of sunflowers so he could be surrounded by a "symphony in blue and yellow."

When Gauguin wrote Van Gogh that he was coming to live with him, Vincent got so excited he made sunflower paintings to decorate Gauguin's bedroom, filling the room with yellow flowers!

Vincent painted irises in a vase and growing in a garden. In the bed of purple irises, one white flower stands alone. The painting represented Vincent's life as an artist. Like the white flower, he was different from everyone around him.

If you painted yourself and others as flowers, what flowers and colours would you choose?

PAUL & VINCENT

In the fall of 1888, Gauguin and Van Gogh lived together in the yellow house. For two months they cooked, ate, and painted together. They also had long discussions about art and their different styles of painting. Vincent made paintings of two chairs. One chair was his and the other was Paul's. Vincent's chair is simple and humble, while Paul's chair is more elegant. Vincent's pipe and tobacco are on his chair. A book and candles are on Paul's. Vincent painted the chairs and the objects on them as symbols of each artist. What do you think he meant to say about himself and his friend?

 Which chair would you choose for yourself?
Choose two items you would put on the chair to describe yourself:
1.   2.

....

Vincent and Paul were friends, but they argued a lot. They often disagreed about art. Vincent was nervous and hard to live with, and he sometimes acted crazy. Paul decided to leave, which made Vincent sad and angry. In a fit, he cut off part of his right earlobe! Paul left Arles and never saw Vincent again, though they wrote letters to each other for the rest of Vincent's life.

Not long after cutting his ear, Vincent painted himself. To show his strong feelings, he chose strong, contrasting colours. Can you find them all?

NIGHT

Vincent's mental illness became worse and worse. His neighbours in Arles were scared of him and complained to the police. He decided to check himself into a nearby hospital. There, Vincent continued to paint. Sometimes he painted scenes he could see from his window; other times he painted from his memory and imagination. New forms began to emerge. In *Starry Night*, he painted huge stars and undulating waves of energy in the night sky. They show his anxieties and also capture the grand beauty of the heavens.

With your finger, trace the waves of energy in the sky.

After a year in the hospital, the doctors discharged him. Vincent moved to a small town north of Paris, called Auvers-sur-Oise. There he became friends with Paul Gachet, a doctor who liked to paint and collect impressionist art. But Vincent still suffered bouts of mental illness. One evening in July 1890, Vincent walked out into a wheat field and shot himself. He died two days later, with his brother Theo by his side.

Dr. Gachet

Vincent Van Gogh was buried in the cemetery in Auvers-sur-Oise, near a church he had painted. The man who hardly sold a single painting in his lifetime was soon recognized as one of the greatest artists of all time.

Text: Catherine de Duve
Graphic design: Kate'Art Editions & Happy Museum!
Concept & coordination: Kate'Art Editions & Happy Museum!
Translation: Wenda O'Reilly, Ph.D.

Photographic credits:
Vincent van Gogh: Amsterdam: Vincent Van Gogh Fondation: *Self-portait*, 1888: pp. 1,12-13 - *The potato eaters*, 1885: pp. 3-5 - *View from Theo's apartment in Paris*, 1887: pp. 3, 6 - *Blossoming almond trees*, 1890: pp. 3, 14 - *Montmartre, The Pepper Mill*, 1887: p. 7 - *Self-portait with straw hat*, 1887: p. 8-9 - *Japonaiserie: Oiran (after Kesaï Eisen)*, 1887: p. 10 - *Japonaiserie: The flowering plum tree (after Hiroshige)*, 1887: p. 10 - *Blossoming almond branch in a glass*,1890: p. 15 - *The Yellow House*, 1888: cover, pp. 16-17 - *The bedroom*, 1888: p. 19 - *Fishing boats on the beach at Saintes-Marie*, 1888: pp. 24 -25 - *Sunflowers*, 1888: cover, p. 26 - *Irises in a vase*, 1890: p. 27 - *Gauguin's chair*, 1888: p. 28 - *Wheat fields with crows*, 1890: p. 31

Otterlo: Kröller-Müller: *The Angelus (after Millet)*, 1880: p. 3 - *Women carrying bags of coal*, 1882: p. 3 - *Peasant woman reaping, seen from the back*, 1885: p. 3 - *The hill of Montmartre*, 1886: p. 3 - *Butte Montmartre*, 1886: p. 6 - *Pink peach trees ('Souvenir de Mauve')*, 1888: p. 15 - *La Berceuse (Portrait of Madame Roulin)*, 1889: p. 22 - *Terrace of a café at night (Place du Forum)*, 1888: pp. 3, 20

Paris: Musée d'Orsay: *Self-portrait*, 1889: p. 2 - *Noontime, rest from work(after Millet)*, 1890: p. 5 - *The Bedroom*, 1888: cover, pp. 3, 18 - *Restaurant de la Sirène in Asnières*, 1887: pp. 3, 6 - *Portrait of Dr. Gachet*, 1890: p. 31 - *The Church at Auvers*, 1890: p. 31 - **Stavros S. Niarchos:** *Portrait of Père Tanguy*, 1887-1888: p. 11

London: Courtauld Institute Gallery: *Self-portrait with bandaged ear*, 1889: p. 9 - **National Gallery:** *Van Gogh's chair*, 1888: p. 28

USA: Washington: National Gallery of Art: *Bulb Fields*, c.1883: p. 3 - **New Haven, Connecticut: Yale University Art Gallery:** *The night café*, 1888: p. 21 - **Los Angeles: The J. Paul Getty Museum:** *Irises*, 1889: cover, p. 27 - **Boston: Museum of Fine Arts:** *Portrait of Joseph Roulin*, 1888: p. 23 - **New York: MET:** *L'Arlésienne (Portrait of Madame Ginoux)*, 1888: p. 22 - **MoMA:** *The starry night*, 1889: p. 30

Private collection: *Self-portrait with bandaged ear*, 1889: p. 29 - *Boats at Saintes-Maries*, 1888: p. 25
Utagawa Hiroshige: *The plum tree, tea-room at Kameido*, 1857: p. 10

With thanks to: Eric Vaes, Julie Stouffs, Priscilla d'Oultremont, Rebecca Gross, Margaret Nab, Kröller-Müller Museum, Otterlo, Suzanne Bogmann, Van Gogh Museum, Amsterdam and everyone who helped to make this book.

http://www.kateart.com